This book belongs to

- -

Help Zero finish the picture by joining up the dots in order.

READING WITH YOUR CHILD

TIPS FOR SHARING THIS BOOK

1 Look at the front cover. What does your child think might happen in the story?

2 Talk about the description on the back cover. Ask your child if they know the difference between an odd and an even number.

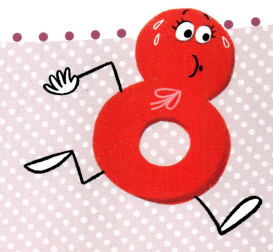

DURING READING

* Encourage your child to describe what is going on in the pictures.

* Ask your child what they think might happen next.

* When you turn the page to see what actually happens, the outcome may or may not be what you expect! Talk about it.

* Encourage your child to count the different objects they can see in the pictures.

* Ask your child to point out which of the Digits are even numbers and which are odd numbers.

* Why can't Zero join one of the teams? Talk about why teams need to have an equal number of players.

* Give your child lots of praise as you go along!

AFTER READING

* Look at the back for some fun activities exploring odd and even numbers

OXFORD
UNIVERSITY PRESS

Great Clarendon Street, Oxford OX2 6DP

Oxford University Press is a department of the University of Oxford.
It furthers the University's objective of excellence in research, scholarship,
and education by publishing worldwide. Oxford is a registered trade mark
of Oxford University Press in the UK and in certain other countries

British Library Cataloguing in Publication Data

Data available

ISBN: 978-0-19-278367-7

1 3 5 7 9 10 8 6 4 2

Printed in China

Paper used in the production of this book is a natural,
recyclable product made from wood grown in sustainable forests.
The manufacturing process conforms to the environmental
regulations of the country of origin.

THE DiGiTS by TONY BRADMAN + SR. SÁNCHEZ

ODDS vs EVENS

OXFORD

UNIVERSITY PRESS

It was a busy Saturday morning at **THE NUMBER TOWER** and the lift was almost full.

'**WAIT FOR ME!**' said Seven, barging Eight out of the way.

'Hey, watch out!' said Four. 'Are you okay, Eight?
That's just typical of you **ODD NUMBERS**, Seven.
You can be so thoughtless sometimes.'

'What are you talking about?' said Seven. 'That's nonsense. **YOU EVEN NUMBERS ARE ALL SO SNOOTY!'**

'I'VE NEVER HEARD SUCH **RUBBISH!'**

shouted Four.

Everyone else joined in, and soon there was . . .

LOTS OF ARGUING.

The **EVENS** were on one side, and the **ODDS** on the other.

Just then Ten arrived, back from an early morning run.

'What's going on?' said Ten. 'Why are you all arguing?'

'It's about who is better, the Evens or the Odds,'
said Four.

'Oh, I see,' said Ten. 'Well, you won't
find out just by shouting at each other.
I know . . . we could have a football
match to sort it out.'

THE DiGiTS all thought it was a **GREAT IDEA** and set off for the park.

'Right, we need to divide into two equal teams,' said Ten.

'That's easy, though — **TEN** is an Even number, so that makes **FIVE** on each side.'
'There you go, I told you that Evens are best!' said Four.
'Really?' said Seven. 'But five is an Odd number . . .'

Ten sent everyone off to get the things they would need for the match.

But Three came back with . . . **THREE** sets of goalposts!

'No, no—we only need **TWO** sets!' said Four. '*SEE—EVENS ARE BEST!*'

'But Two has brought **TWO** footballs—and we only need **ONE!**' said Seven. 'So actually, it looks to me like **ODD NUMBERS ARE BEST!**'

Four was just about to start complaining again, but then Zero turned up.
'So, this is where you all are!' said Zero. 'Which team am I playing for?'

'Er, sorry, Zero,' said Ten. 'We've got just the right number of players on each side. So, I'm afraid you won't be playing for either team . . .'
Suddenly, Zero looked very sad.

'...But would you like to be the referee?' Ten went on.
'You'll be in charge ...'

'And you'll also have a whistle to blow,' said Nine. 'Here it is!'
'Whoa, that is so cool!' said Zero. 'Let's get this game started!'
'Here we go!' said One.

The game was **VERY EXCITING**.

After a while, Eight took a shot at goal . . .

and the ball flew past Seven!

GOAL!   The Evens were in the lead!

Seven was cross and started chewing a goalpost.

The Odds swept down the pitch.

Two was too busy eating grass to notice that
Nine was about to take a shot . . .

but Ten **BLOCKED** it!

'That's a double foul!' said Zero, blowing the whistle. 'Eating the grass isn't allowed! And you can't block a shot like that, Ten—it's not fair!'

'I think you just like blowing your whistle,' muttered Seven.

After that, things got very hectic. The Odds scored . . .

the Evens scored . . .

and then the Odds scored again. It was **TWO ALL!**

Six passed the ball to Four, who ran towards the goal.

Four only had to get the ball past Seven for the Evens to win the game.

Four kept running and hit
A TERRIFIC SHOT!
Four was sure it
was going in.

But Seven leapt up . . . and made an **ABSOLUTELY AMAZING SAVE!**

'**NOooo!**' cried Four.

Zero blew the whistle.
'I declare this game . . . **A DRAW!**'

'Oh no,' groaned Four.
'We were so close to winning!'

But then Four looked round and saw that
everyone was laughing and hugging.
'Well, that was a lot of fun,' said Seven.
'It's great when we play together.'

'You're right,' said Four. 'Odds and Evens
are **BOTH** better . . . when they play together.
Three cheers for everyone!'

And Zero blew the whistle all the way back to The Number Tower!

ACTIVITIES

THE TOWER GAME

1 Give your child a random number of evenly sized building blocks.

2 Ask them if they can build two towers the same height.

3 If they manage to build two towers the same height, it means they have an even number of blocks altogether. If they end up with a tower that's a block taller than the other, that means they have an odd number of blocks.

4 Count the total number of blocks in the two towers.

5 Have fun knocking the towers down and starting again!

LET'S SHARE!

1   Place ten pebbles or dried beans in a cloth bag.

2   Ask your child to pull out a handful of pebbles or beans.

3   Can they share them out equally between the two of you? If so, it means they picked up an even number. If not, it means it was an odd number.

4   Count how many pebbles or beans you have altogether.

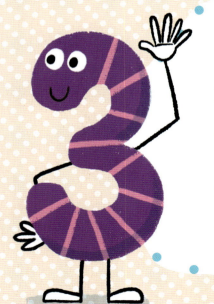

OUT AND ABOUT

Even numbers always end with a 0, 2, 4, 6 or 8, and odd numbers always end with 1, 3, 5, 7 or 9. When you are out and about, look out for numbers on houses, buses, signs, and in shops. Ask your child if it's an odd or even number.